20
Fun-Filled Games That Build Early Reading Skills

Quick & Easy Literacy Games That Get Emergent Readers Off to a Great Start!

by

Caroline Linse

SCHOLASTIC
PROFESSIONAL BOOKS

NEW YORK • TORONTO • LONDON • AUCKLAND • SYDNEY
MEXICO CITY • NEW DELHI • HONG KONG

Dedication
To Fran and the Early Childhood Center,
American School Foundation, Mexico City for modeling stellar education.

Acknowledgments
This book would not have been possible without wonderful students and
teachers scattered throughout the globe in Korea, Hungary, Guadalajara, Mexico,
North Carolina, Maine, Massachusetts and Rhode Island.

Cover design by Pamela Simmons
Cover artwork by Shelley Dieterichs
Interior design by Solutions by Design, Inc.
Interior artwork by Margeaux Lucas

ISBN: 0-439-16520-2

Contents

Introduction   4

GAME TITLE	SKILL AREA	PAGE
Alphabet Red Light, Green Light	vowels and consonants	7
Blends Go Fish!	sound blends	8
Hide the Digraphs	digraphs	12
Color and Shape Word Race	color and shape words	15
Initial-Sound Board Game	initial sounds and letters	19
Letter-Sound Bingo	initial sounds and letters	23
Read-the-Message Simon Says	simple commands	26
Word and Shape Matchups	word configurations	29
End-Sound Snake Around	final sounds	34
Two-Letter Switcheroo	letter names	39
Tongue Twister Challenge	initial sounds	43
Sight-Word Scurry	number words	44
Spell-and-Tell Word Race	letters of the alphabet	47
Read, Write, and Win	simple words	49
Calendar Words Tic-Tac-Toe	days and months	51
Opposite-Word Concentration	opposite meaning	54
Rhyming Words Relay	rhyming words	57
Word-Match Dominoes	rhyming words	58
Vowel Dice Toss	long and short vowels	63
Collaborative Crossword Puzzle	Dolch words	65
Reproducible Templates		69

Introduction

Dear Friends,

Children like to play games at home, in the car, on the playground, and in the classroom. Why not use fun, skill-building games to reinforce basic concepts? When children play the games in this book, they hardly realize that they are learning and not just having a good time.

In this book, you will find 20 games designed to help children develop and reinforce their emergent literacy skills, in both basic phonetic awareness and sight word recognition. As your students play these games, they will gain proficiency in identifying letters and sounds, consonants and short and long vowels, words that rhyme, and words both related and opposite in meaning. They will also have valuable practice in reading and vocabulary building. Incidentally, in developing these games I kept in mind the needs of children learning English as a second or foreign language.

The games, for the most part, are variations of favorite childhood games children play purely for recreational purposes. For example, Simon Says becomes Read-the-Message Simon Says, a game in which "Simon Says" and the commands are displayed as written words that children have to read. Go Fish concentrates on blends. The game Tic–Tac–Toe is used to help children practice reading the days of the week and the months of the year.

Preparing the Games

Many of the games require nothing more than simple classroom materials such as paper and pencil. For other games you will need game-playing pieces and game boards. Reproducible templates are included with the necessary game cards and cutouts for game boards and playing pieces. Playing pieces immediately follow the general instructions for each game.

The number of students who can play each game is flexible. For example, many games that are normally played by several groups of children at the same time can be adapted to smaller group settings. The number range of players listed for each game allows for such adaptations.

Some of the games require a "first player" to be chosen. You may wish to decide in advance what strategy or strategies you will use for such choices—for example, asking for volunteers, taking turns around the class, or some method involving chance. For games that require score keeping, you may also wish to decide in advance how that will be done.

In games that encourage children to venture correct answers, consider setting up simple routines. For instance, if a child answers a question incorrectly, pause game playing. Invite all students to work together to determine the correct answer.

Using the Games

There are many different ways to incorporate game-making and game-playing into your daily curriculum. All of the games can be used as a reward for completing one's work. Those that do not require any materials can usually be played with the whole class and are a great way to practice skills during a five- or ten-minute period of time.

Other games can be set up in learning centers. You may wish to have a game-playing center that children go to during their literacy block or when they have finished their other work. The game center can be an independent center, or it can be staffed by a parent, school volunteer, or paraprofessional. Store the games in file folders or in large manila envelopes. You may wish to rotate the games in the learning center.

Link families and children, home and school with the fun, learning-filled games in this book. You'll find lots of the game boards and card games can easily be sent home with children for the whole family to play. Encourage students to teach their families the basic rules of the games.

Making More Games

Children delight in making their own games. At the end of this book, you will find templates for making Bingo, Concentration, and Go Fish games, and collaborative crossword puzzles. You simply supply your own information and follow the instructions with the model games shared in the book.

I hope that you and your students enjoy playing the games in this book. Have fun!

Best wishes,
Caroline Linse

Alphabet Red Light, Green Light

This is a simple variation of the childhood-favorite game,
Red Light, Green Light.

Objective: To practice identifying vowels and consonants.

Players: 2 to 30 children

Materials: none

Preparation: Review vowels and consonants with students.

To Play the Game

1 Have children line up against a wall facing you. You should be five to ten feet away from students.

2 Tell students that you are going to say consonants and vowels. If they hear a consonant, they freeze. If they hear a vowel, they take a baby-step forward.

3 Say consonants and vowels randomly until a student reaches you. That student is the winner.

Variation

✢ Have different students play the role of the leader.

Blends Go Fish!

This is a variation of the childhood favorite, Go Fish.

Objective: To practice identifying matching sound blends.

Players: 2 to 4 children

Materials: Go Fish! game cards

Preparation: Cut out the Blends Go Fish! game cards. You may wish to laminate the cards or cover them with contact paper.

To Play the Game

1 Explain that the purpose of the game is to get as many pairs as possible. A pair is two cards with the same sound blend.

2 Shuffle the cards. Deal four cards to each player and put the remaining cards in a pile. Remind children to hold their cards so that other players cannot see them.

3 Have each child put all cards that begin with the same letter together. Pairs of cards with the same sound blend may be placed in a separate pile.

4 The first player chooses a blend from his or her hand and asks another player if s/he has a card that starts with that blend. For example, the first player might ask for a card starting with the *br* blend.

5 If the second player has a word that starts with the requested blend, s/he gives it to the first player. The first player places the pair in a separate pile and asks for another card in the same way. Note: If the second player does not possess a card with the requested blend s/he says, "Go fish!" The first player then draws a card from the pile. If the card drawn creates a pair, the first player may place the pair in his or her pile.

6 The second player repeats the process. Play continues until all the cards in the "go fish" pile are gone. The winner is the child with the most pairs of cards.

Variations

✛ This game can be played with partners. Assign two players or partners to each set of cards.

✛ Make your own Go Fish! game cards using the template on page 72.

20 Fun-Filled Games That Build Early Reading Skills Scholastic Professional Books

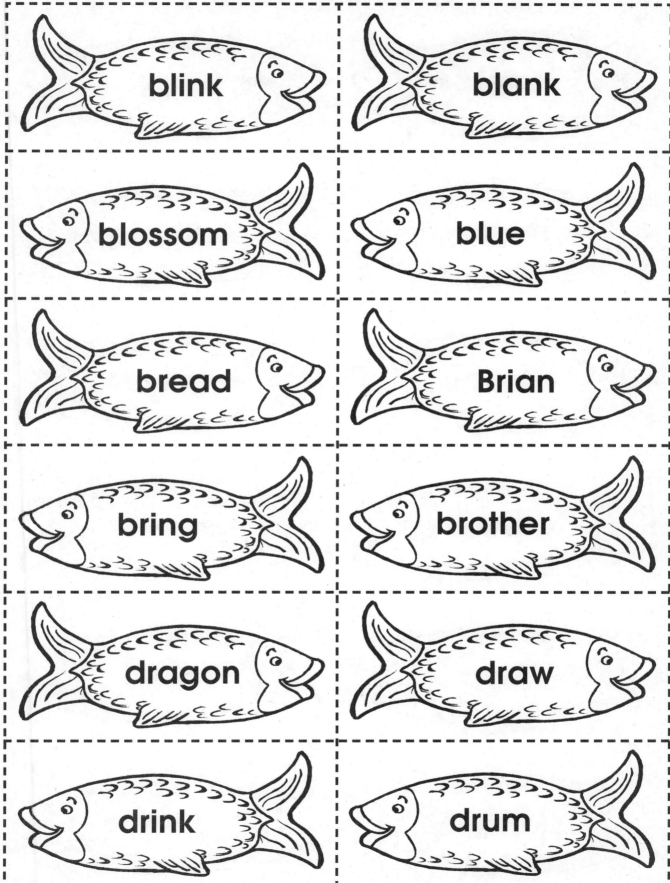

blink

blank

blossom

blue

bread

Brian

bring

brother

dragon

draw

drink

drum

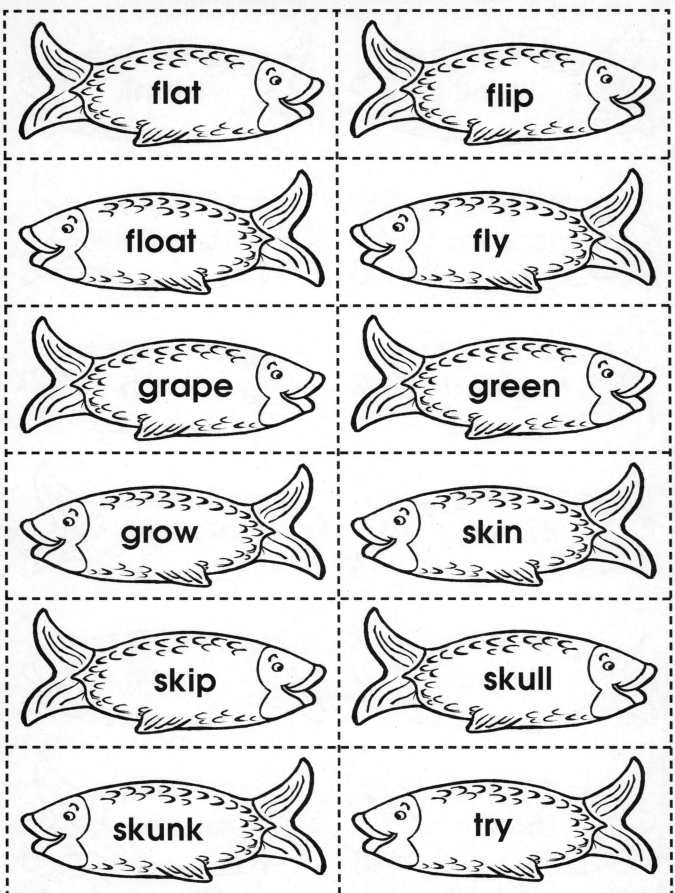

flat

flip

float

fly

grape

green

grow

skin

skip

skull

skunk

try

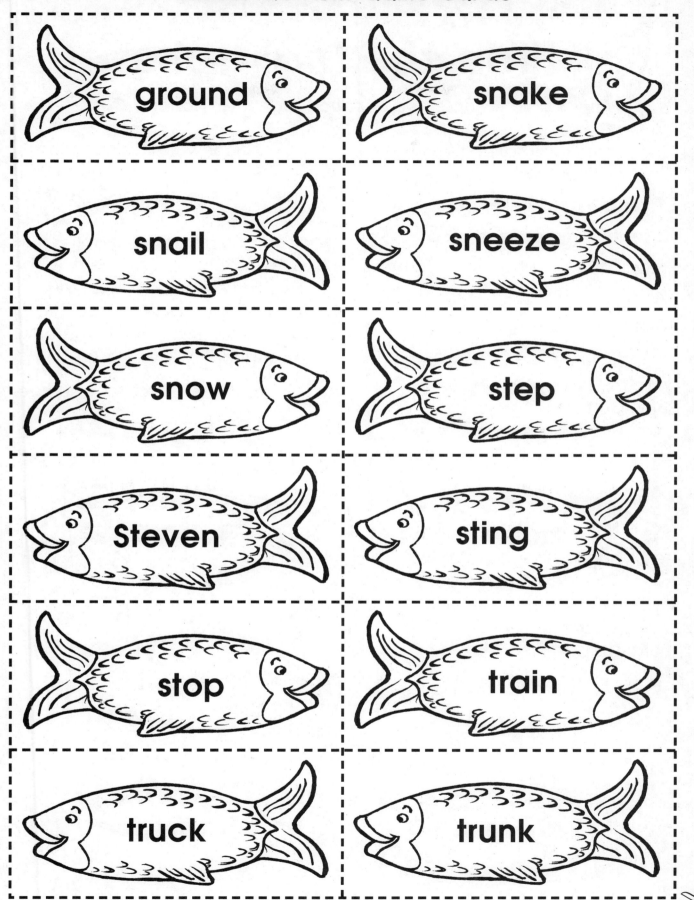

ground

snake

snail

sneeze

snow

step

Steven

sting

stop

train

truck

trunk

Hide the Digraphs

This is a variation of the childhood favorite, Hot and Cold.

Objective: To practice reading words with digraphs.

Players: 4 to 30 children

Materials: digraph word cards

Preparation: Cut out the digraph word cards.

To Play the Game

1 Review the digraphs *sh*, *ch*, *th*, and *wh* with students. Show students a digraph word card. Have students sound out the digraph and read the word aloud.

2 Ask a volunteer to leave the room. While the volunteer is out of the room, have students help you hide the digraph word card in a place that is slightly visible. All of the children in the class need to know where the word has been hidden.

3 Bring the volunteer back to the classroom, and have him or her try to find the card. The rest of the class gives hints by chanting the sound and the word (for example, "Ch, ch, ch, cherry"). The class chants more loudly as the volunteer gets closer to the card and more softly as the volunteer moves farther away.

4 Continue with other volunteer "hunters."

20 Fun-Filled Games That Build Early Reading Skills **Scholastic Professional Books**

shape	sheep
shirt	shot
shy	chant
Charles	chart
chain	cheese
cherry	chicken

child	thanks
that	think
thunder	Thursday
whale	wheel
while	whisper
whistle	white

20 Fun-Filled Games That Build Early Reading Skills Scholastic Professional Books

Color and Shape Word Race

This is a simple board game that helps children practice identifying shape and color words.

Objective: To practice identifying shape and color words.

Players: 2 to 6 children

Materials: game board, crayons, game markers, one die (The game can also be played with two dice.)

Preparation: Put the two reproducible pages together to make the circular game board. Color the spaces as indicated.

To Play the Game

1 Have each player select a game-playing piece: Smiler, Singer, Dancer, Runner, Jumper, Flier. Each child puts his or her marker on the **Start** space.

2 The first player rolls the die and moves forward. The player reads the words in the space. The player remains on the space unless there are instructions to move forward or back. If the player moves, s/he also reads the words in the new space.

3 Continue with the following players. The winner is the first player to reach the space labeled **Win**. Children do not need an exact count to win. For example, if a player needs a 3 to win and throws a 4 on the die, the player still wins.

Variations

✛ This game can be played with partners. Assign two players or partners to each marker.

✛ You can make quiet dice by cutting a cube from a sponge and marking the dots on each side.

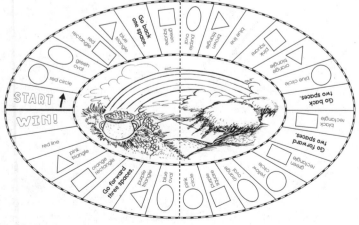

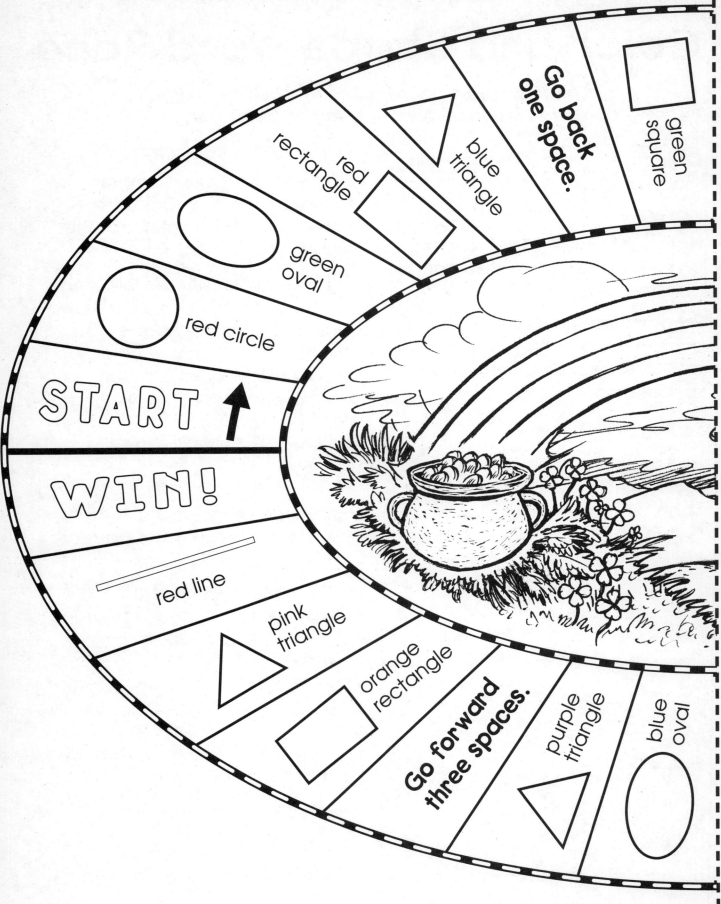

green square

Go back one space.

blue triangle

red rectangle

green oval

red circle

START ↑

WIN!

red line

pink triangle

orange rectangle

Go forward three spaces.

purple triangle

blue oval

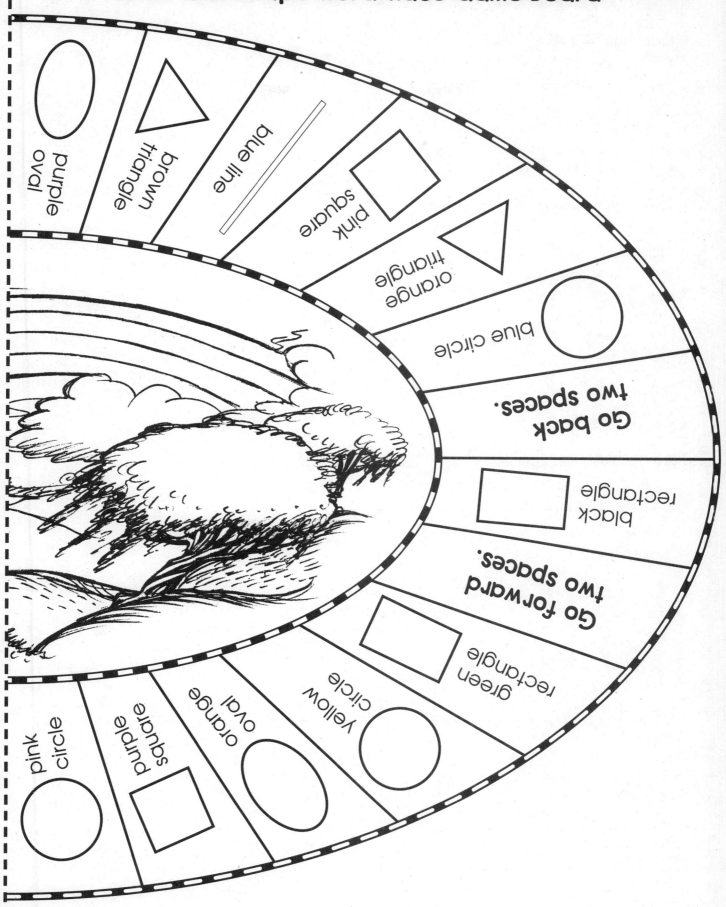

purple oval

brown triangle

blue line

pink square

orange triangle

blue circle

Go back two spaces.

black rectangle

Go forward two spaces.

green rectangle

yellow circle

orange oval

purple square

pink circle

Preparation of Markers

1. Photocopy this page.

2. Cut out the markers and their bases.

3. Glue the figures and bases to posterboard for durability.

4. Cut along the dotted lines at the bottom of each marker and at the top of each base.

5. Assemble the markers as shown here.

Smiley

Singer

Runner

Dancer

Jumper

Flier

Initial-Sound Board Game

This is a simple board game that helps children practice identifying initial sounds and letters.

Objective: To practice identifying initial sounds and letters.

Players: 2 to 4 children

Materials: game board, game markers, penny, small piece of red construction paper, small piece of green construction paper, glue stick

Preparation: Put the two reproducible pages together to make the game board. Cover one side of a penny with a red piece of paper and the other side with a green piece of paper.

To Play the Game

1 Explain to players that they'll need to say a word that names the picture their pieces land on. Every player needs to listen closely to the word and think about the first sound they hear.

2 Have each player select a game piece marker: Dog, Dragon, Dinosaur, or Monster. Each child puts his or her marker on a different **Start** space.

3 The first player flips the prepared penny. If the color green is faceup, the player moves one space forward and identifies the beginning letter and/or sound of the name of the pictured object. If the color red is faceup, the student does not move forward.

4 If the player incorrectly identifies the letter and/or sound, play pauses. All players work together to determine the initial sound and/or letter.

5 Continue with other players. The winner is the first player to reach the **Winner's Circle**.

Variation

✤ This game can be played with partners. Assign two players or partners to each marker.

Preparation of Markers

1. Photocopy this page.

2. Cut out the markers and their bases.

3. Glue the figures and bases to posterboard for durability.

4. Cut along the dotted lines at the bottom of each marker and at the top of each base.

5. Assemble the markers as shown here.

Letter-Sound Bingo

This is a simple variation of the favorite game, Bingo.

Objective: To practice identifying initial sounds and letters.

Players: 2 to 6 children

Materials: Bingo cards, calling cards, construction paper

Preparation:

✤ Cut out the Bingo cards and the letter-sound calling cards.

✤ Cut out, or have students cut out, ten pieces of construction paper each as markers. The markers should be approximately $1/2$" square.

To Play the Game

1 Pass out one Bingo card to each student. Make sure each student has a set of ten markers.

2 Tell students that they should put a marker on the space with the word **FREE**.

3 Explain that you are going to say letters and their sounds. Each time you say a letter and sound, students should look to see if they have a picture of something that begins with that letter and sound. If so, they are to put a marker on the picture. For example, if you say "f" and they have a picture of a fish, they should put a marker on the picture of the fish. Once a child has markers in a line on spaces going up and down, or across (including the FREE space), s/he is to call out "Bingo!"

4 Turn up the first calling card, say the letter printed on it, and make the sound. Continue turning up calling cards and saying letters/sounds until a student calls "Bingo!" That student is the winner.

Variations

✤ To increase the number of players, have two students share one Bingo card.

✤ Make copies of the blank Bingo card on page 69 to create your own Bingo games.

✤ Give older students the option calling "Bingo!" when the markers form a diagonal line on the game board.

Letter-Sound Bingo Cards

(nose)	(moon)	(hand)
(pants)	FREE	(cat)
5	(hat)	(leaf)

Letter-Sound Bingo Cards

(broom)	(balloon)	(sailboat)
(fish)	FREE	(necklace)
(mouse)	(tiger)	(dog)

Letter-Sound Bingo Cards

(watch)	(lion)	(button)
(fork)	FREE	(sock)
(pillow)	(milk carton)	(towel)

Letter-Sound Bingo Cards

(foot)	(nail)	(baseball)
7	FREE	(rain cloud)
(donut)	(boat)	(foot)

Letter-Sound Bingo Cards

(sun)	(nail)	(carrot)
(ring)	FREE	(book)
(pen)	(mouth)	(window)

Letter-Sound Bingo Cards

(pajamas)	(globe)	(lips)
4	FREE	(dog)
(queen)	(salt shaker)	(man)

20 Fun-Filled Games That Build Early Reading Skills Scholastic Professional Books

Bb	**Nn**
Cc	**Pp**
Dd	**Qq**
Ff	**Rr**
Hh	**Ss**
Ll	**Tt**
Mm	**Ww**

Read-the-Message
Simon Says

This game combines early literacy with the childhood favorite, Simon Says.

Objective: To practice reading and following simple commands.

Players: 2 to 30 children

Materials: Simon Says Calling Cards

Preparation: Cut apart the command cards.

To Play the Game

1 Let the students see the cards before starting the game.

2 Explain to the children that this is a variation of the game Simon Says. You will not say any words at all. Instead, you will show a card that is either blank or has the words "Simon Says" on it, and then you will show one of the command cards. If you show the "Simon Says" card first, students are to follow the command all at once. If you show the blank card first, students are to remain still.

3 Play continues until the "Clap your hands" card is shown.

Variations

⊕ Create a list of your own command cards.

⊕ Let students take turns as leader.

20 Fun-Filled Games That Build Early Reading Skills Scholastic Professional Books

Raise your hand.

Touch your head.

Whisper your name.

Say, "Hello."

Wave.

Say, "Good-bye."

Point to the window.

Knock on the table.

Open your mouth.

Close your eyes.

Stand up.

Sit down.

Point to the door.

Walk.

Cry.

Laugh.

Touch your foot.

Smile.

Wiggle your nose.

Clap your hands.

(blank)

Simon Says

20 Fun-Filled Games That Build Early Reading Skills Scholastic Professional Books

Word and Shape Matchups

This game helps children develop sight-reading skills.

Objectives: To identify the configurations of written words.

Players: 2 to 4 children in each team. The game can be played with up to 5 teams.

Materials: word cards and word shape cards

Preparation: Cut out the word cards and word-shape cards.

To Play the Game

1 Explain that the children will try to match written words with their shape or outline as quickly as possible. As an example, you might write a word and draw its shape on the chalkboard or a large piece of paper.

2 Give each team a set of words from one of the five categories noted below. Have the teams match the word-shape cards and the word cards in thirty seconds or less. The team that can correctly match the word cards and word-shape cards the fastest is the winner.

Variation

✛ If you limit the number of teams to just a few, you can record each team's completion time. After a few rounds, add the times of each team. The one with the shortest total time is the winner.

Fruit	Clothes	Food	People	Things in a House
cherry	shirt	butter	mother	lamp
lemon	shoe	tortilla	father	table
orange	sock	bread	sister	bed
apple	pants	hot dog	brother	chair
banana	dress	salad	uncle	sofa
grape			aunt	book

cherry

lemon

orange

apple

banana

shirt

shoe

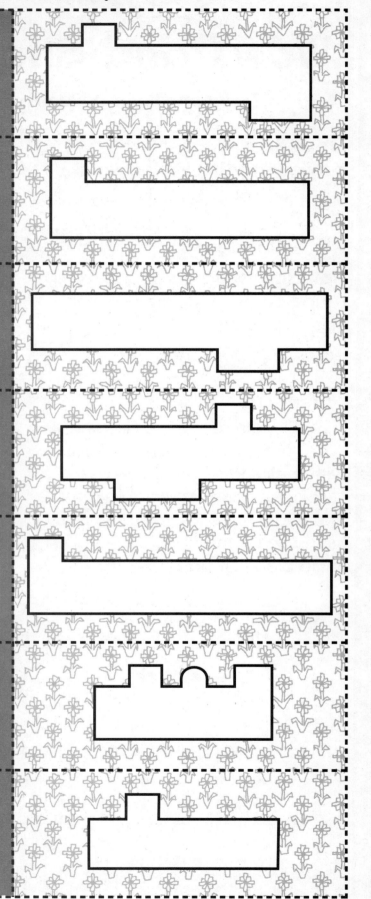

Word and Shape Matchups Cards

sock

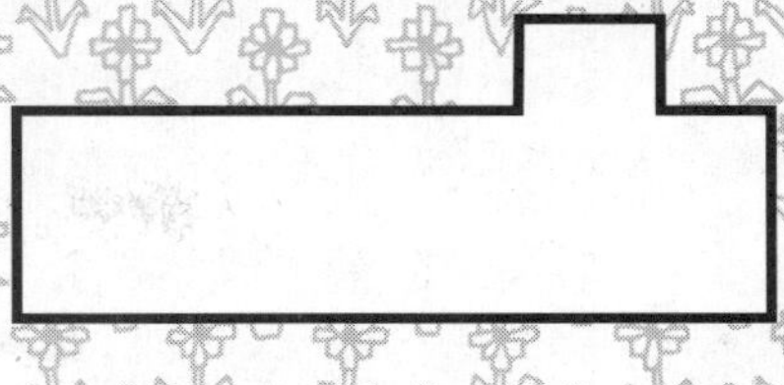

pants

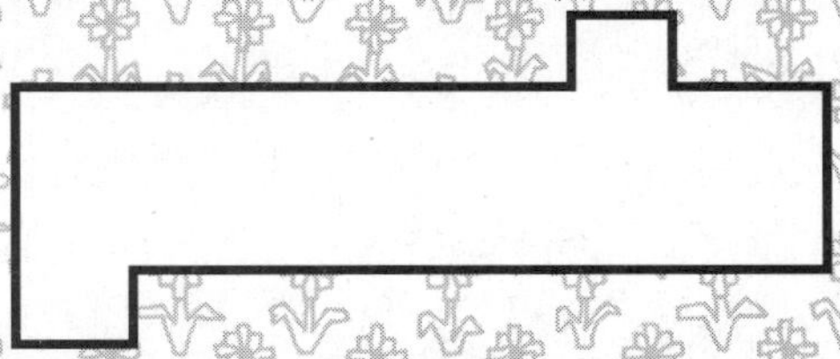

dress

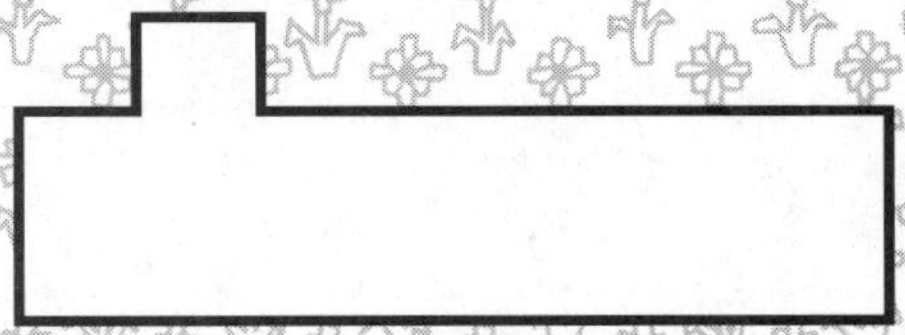

butter

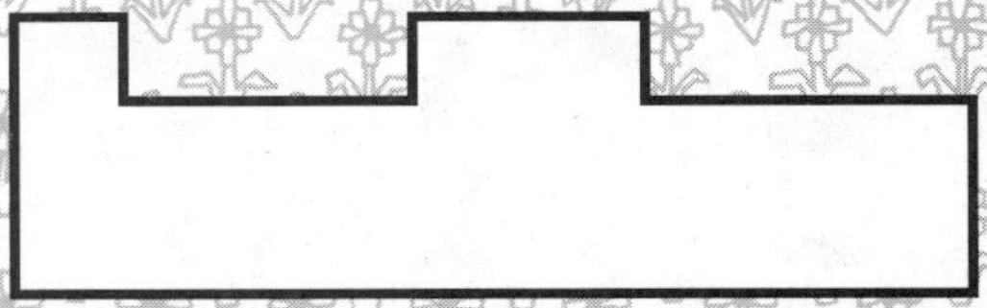

tortilla

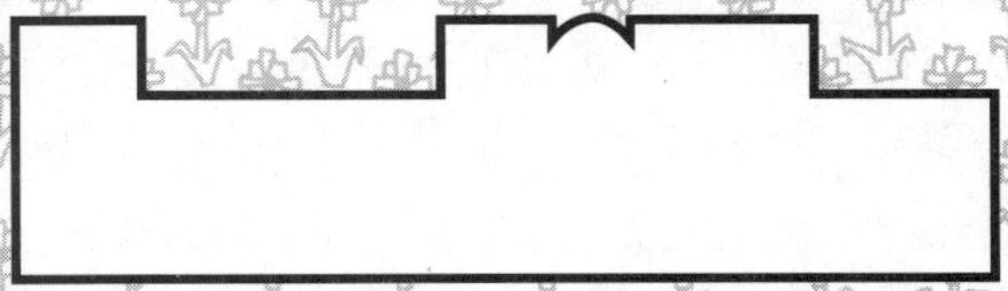

bread

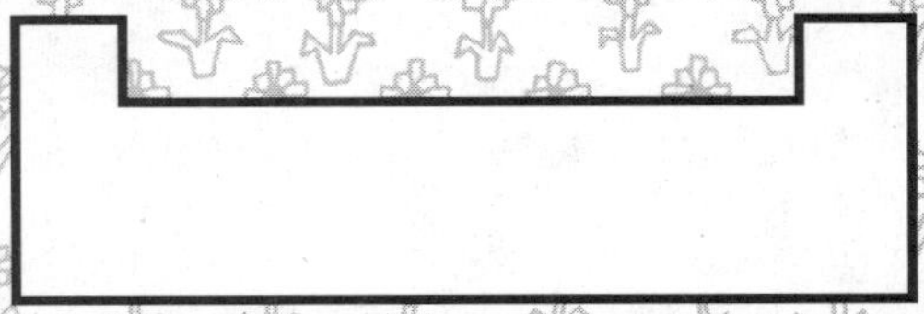

hot dog

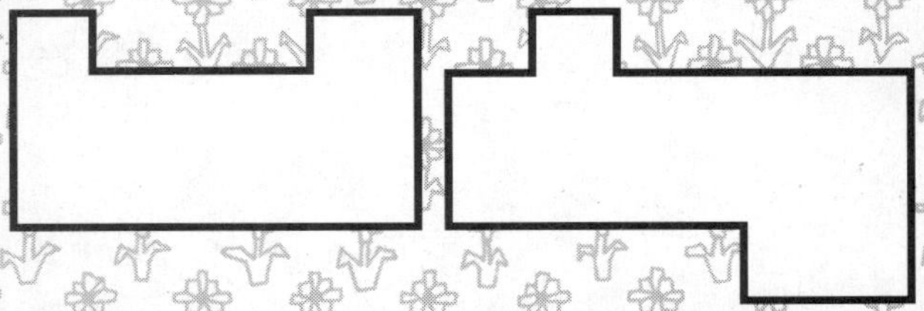

salad

mother

father

sister

brother

uncle

lamp

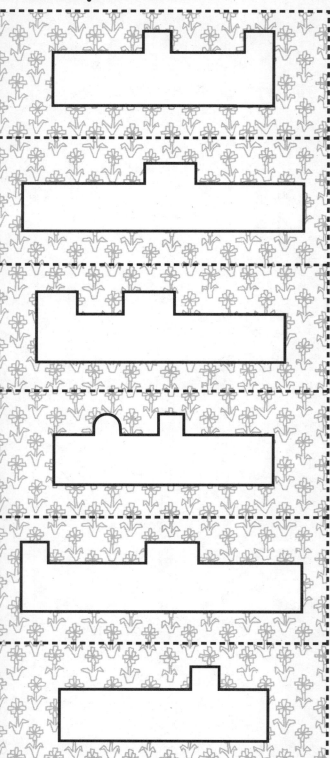

table

bed

chair

sofa

aunt

book

grape

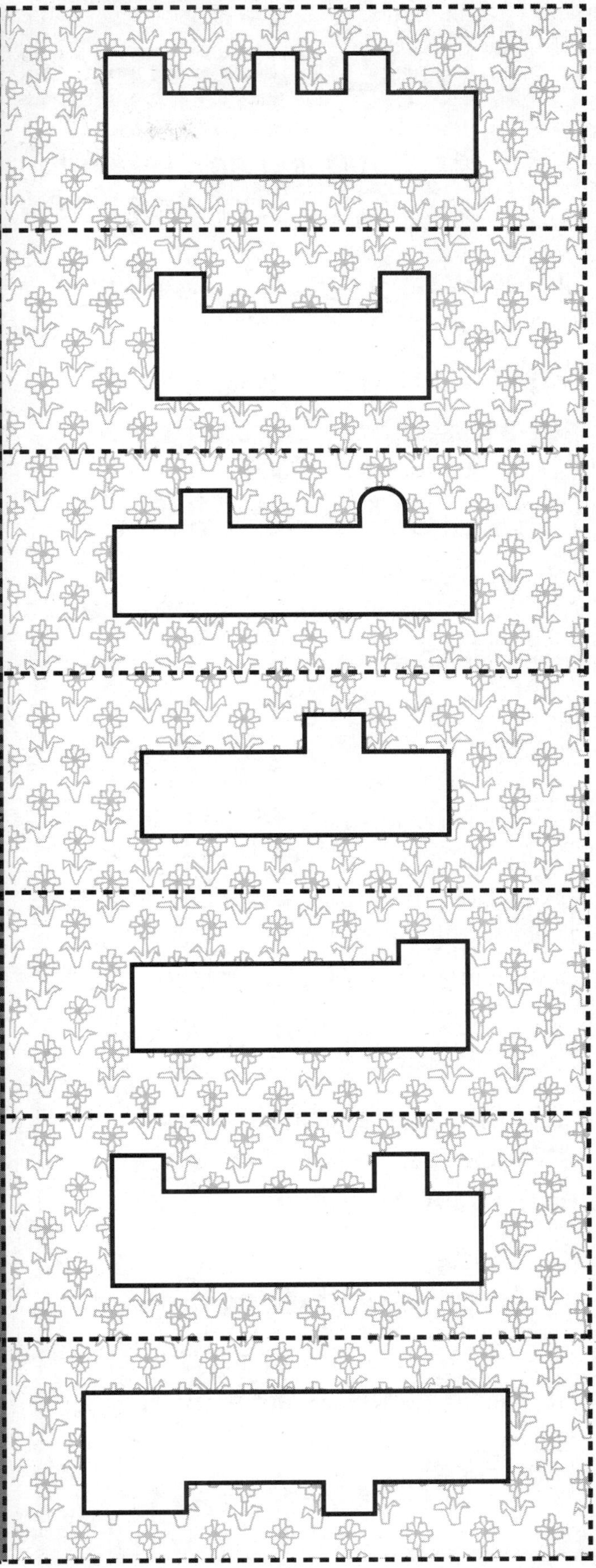

End-Sound Snake Around

This is a simple board game that helps children practice identifying final sounds.

Objective: To practice identifying final sounds.

Players: 2 to 6 children

Materials: game board, game markers, game cards

Preparation: Put the two reproducible pages together to make the snake. Cut out the game cards and markers.

To Play the Game

1 Have each player select a game-playing piece: Elephant, Lion, Rhinoceros, Zebra, Giraffe, Leopard. You might explain to the children that these animals (and the snake on the board) are found not only in zoos, but in their home on the African grasslands.

2 Place the game cards facedown on the space marked **Game Cards**.

3 Have each child put his or her marker on the **Begin** space.

4 Each player in turn draws a game card and moves accordingly. If the game card shows a plus number (such as +3), the student goes forward the same number of spaces and identifies the ending sound of the word pictured. If the game card shows a minus number (such as -1), the student goes backward that number of spaces (except on the first move, when s/he remains on the **Begin** space) and also identifies the ending sound. The student remains in place if the card shows 0.

5 Play continues until one student reaches the head of the snake.

Note: If a player misidentifies the ending sound, you may choose whether to prompt a correction or impose a penalty such as moving back one space.

Variations

✥ Assign two players or partners to each marker.

✥ Invite players to work together to determine the final sounds.

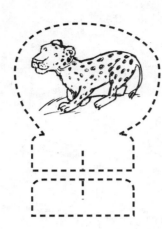

Preparation of Markers

1. Photocopy this page.

2. Cut out the markers and their bases.

3. Glue the figures and bases to posterboard for durability.

4. Cut along the dotted lines at the bottom of each marker and at the top of each base.

5. Assemble the markers as shown here.

Game Cards

+4	**+3**	**+4**	**+3**
-1	**+1**	**-1**	**+1**
+1	**+2**	**+1**	**+2**
+2	**-2**	**+2**	**-2**
+3	**0**	**+3**	**0**

20 Fun-Filled Games That Build Early Reading Skills Scholastic Professional Books

Two-Letter Switcheroo

This is a variation of the childhood game, Fruit-Basket Upset.

Objective: To practice identifying letter names.

Players: 3 to 25 children

Materials: letter cards

Preparation: Cut out the letter cards.

To Play the Game

1 Place chairs in a circle. There should be only one chair for each student.

2 Give each child a letter card. Have children sit in the chairs. Ask them to look at their cards and remember the letter on their card. Then ask them to hold their letter cards facing toward the center of the circle.

3 Stand in the center of the circle. Explain that you will call two different letters. The students holding the letters must then change places. They should do it as quickly as possible because you will try to sit on one of the chairs!

4 Look at the letters being held. Call two different letters. As the students holding those letters change places, sit on one of the chairs vacated so that one student is left standing in the middle. (If you wish, you can let the students win this time.)

5 The student in the middle looks at the letters being held and calls two more letters. This time the caller tries to sit on one of the vacated chairs.

6 The game continues in the same way for as long as you wish.

Variations

- Give students the option of calling "all vowels" or "all consonants." All of the students holding vowel cards or all of the students holding consonant cards then change places.

- Cut apart the letters to create a set of uppercase cards or a set of lowercase cards. You may wish to draw small happy faces on the lowercase b, d, p and q to help avoid confusion. The happy faces will help children orient the letters more easily.

A a   F f

B b   G g

C c   H h

D d   I i

E e   J j

Kk Pp

Ll Qq

Mm Rr

Nn Ss

Oo Tt

U u X x

V v Y y

W w Z z

Tongue Twister Challenge

This simple game helps children create their own tongue twisters.

Objective: To practice identifying words that have the same initial sounds.

Players: 10 to 30 children

Materials: index cards, list of 15 to 20 words students are currently studying

Preparation: Print words on index cards that students are studying. Print one word on each card.

To Play the Game

1 Have students stand in a circle. The first player takes the top card and reads the word—for example, "dog." The second player says the first player's word and adds a second word that starts with same sound—for example, "dog, Dave."

2 Continue with as many players and as many words that start with the same sound as children can identify (or remember). After each new word, the entire class chants the chain of words so far. Encourage the children to see how quickly they can say or chant the word sequence—which will be a tongue twister!

3 Continue with another round, making sure that the new word has a different starting sound. The game can continue as long as the children enjoy it, so that all of them are winners.

Variation

✤ Have children write down the tongue twisters that they have created with the add-on game. These tongue twisters can be used as the basis of student-made tongue-twister booklets.

Sight-Word Scurry

This is a simple variation of the childhood game, Steal the Bacon.

Objective: To practice identifying number sight words.

Players: 2 to 30 children

Materials: number sight-word cards

Preparation: Cut apart the number sight-word cards. You may want to mount them on tagboard or card stock and laminate them.

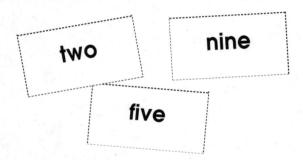

To Play the Game

1 Divide students into two teams. Have the teams line up facing each other several feet apart. (The farther apart they are, the more activity there will be.) Place the number sight words (in random order) faceup on the floor between the teams. Designate the order of players for each team.

2 Tell students that you will be calling out numbers. When you call the first number, the first player of each team is to try to touch the number card before the other one does. For example, if you say "eighteen," the first player of each team should rush to touch the eighteen number card. The team of the student who first touches the card keeps it.

3 Continue the same procedure with the other pairs of players on each team. The winning team is the one with the most cards at the end of the game.

Variation

⚙ Play the same game using other picture and word cards.

one	six
two	seven
three	eight
four	nine
five	ten

eleven	sixteen
twelve	seventeen
thirteen	eighteen
fourteen	nineteen
fifteen	twenty

20 Fun-Filled Games That Build Early Reading Skills Scholastic Professional Books

Spell-and-Tell Word Race

This game gives children practice with dictation, one letter at a time.

Objectives:

To identify letters of the alphabet.

To use letters to form words.

To identify groups of words belonging to one category.

Players: 2 to 30 children

Materials: list of categories of words (See page 48.)

Preparation: Students will need paper and pencils.

To Play the Game

1 Have each child write the numbers 1 to 5 down the left side of his or her piece of paper. Explain to students that they are going to print five words, one letter at a time. Students are to figure out the words and the category or group the words belong to.

2 Dictate the words letter by letter. For example, "One: c - a - t." Then ask, "What word is it?" Continue with the other words (in this case *dog*, *pig*, *hen*, and *goat*). Ask, "What are these words? How are they like one another?" Encourage children to respond, "They are all animals."

3 Continue with other word groups. If you wish to make the game competitive, the first child to identify the group is the winner for that round.

Variation

✛ Use other words that students are currently studying.

Animals	Clothes	School Supplies	Parts of the Face	Parts of the Body
cat	hat	pen	nose	leg
dog	coat	paper	eye	arm
hen	sock	book	ear	hand
pig	skirt	pencil	lip	head
goat	dress	ruler	mouth	foot

Fruits	Vegetables	Nature	Things You Use to Eat and Drink	Transportation
apple	corn	flower	plate	car
pear	carrots	tree	cup	bus
grape	peas	sky	glass	train
orange	beans	sun	knife	truck
banana	lettuce	moon	fork	boat

Read, Write, and Win

This is a written variation of the childhood favorite, Grapevine (or Telephone).

Objective: To practice memorizing and copying simple words.

Players: 4 to 30 children

Materials: index cards, list of 15 to 20 words that students are currently studying

Preparation: On index cards, print words that the children are studying. Print one word on each card, but print as many cards for each word as there are teams (see direction #1 below).

To Play the Game

1. Divide the class into teams of five to seven students each. (With a very small number of students, have one "team" and play just for fun.) Have each team sit in a row as pictured on page 50. Give each child a blank index card.

2. Using cards with the same word printed on them, place one of the prepared index cards facedown in front of the first player of each team. Explain that players will have only one second to see what is printed on a card, starting with the teams' first players. You will cue them when to turn the card over and when to turn it down.

3. Tell each first player, "Turn the card over," and one second later, "Turn the card down." Each first player writes on the blank card what s/he saw on the printed card.

4. Now explain that each first player will show the word s/he has just written to the second player for one second. The second player will write down what he or she saw printed on the card.

5. Tell each second player, "Show the card," and one second later, "Stop showing." Continue with the rest of the players on each team. The winning team is the one whose last word most closely matches the first.

Calendar Words Tic-Tac-Toe

This game combines sight-word learning with the childhood favorite, Tic-Tac-Toe.

Objective: To practice reading days of the week and months of the year.

Players: 2 to 30 children

Materials: calendar sight-word cards, masking tape

Preparation: Draw a large tic-tac-toe-style board on the chalkboard. Print a numeral between 1 and 9 in each space. Tape one of the month or day-of-the-week sight-word cards under the number in each space.

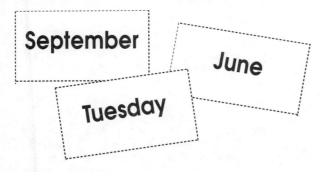

To Play the Game

1 Divide the class into two teams: team **X** and team **O**. The aim for each team is to have three **X**'s or **O**'s across, down, or diagonally before the other team. At each turn, three team members play or participate in the game.

2 Team **X** begins the game. Team member 1 picks a number. Team member 2 reads the word. Team member 3 uses the word in a sentence.

3 If all three team members respond correctly, the team writes an **X** in the square selected. If the answer is incorrect, the square remains blank.

4 Three members of team **O** take their turn.

5 Three different members of each team now take turns. The winning team is the first team to have three **X**'s or three **O**'s in a row.

Variation

✢ Use words from students' content areas.

January	June
February	July
March	August
April	September
May	October

November	**Thursday**
December	**Friday**
Monday	**Saturday**
Tuesday	**Sunday**
Wednesday	

Opposite-Word Concentration

This is a variation of childhood favorite, Concentration.

Objectives: To practice learning words with opposite meanings.
To increase visual memory skills.

Players: 2 to 5 children

Materials: opposite-word picture cards, optional 5" x 8" index cards

Preparation: Cut out the opposite-word picture cards. You may wish to mount them on 5" x 8" index cards. Stack the cards and place them facedown on a table or the floor.

To Play the Game

1 Ask students to shuffle the cards and lay them facedown in rows.

2 Players take turns turning over two cards at a time, looking for two words with opposite meanings. When a player finds two cards with opposite meanings, s/he may take another turn.

3 Continue with other players until all of the cards have been matched. The winner is the child with the most cards at the end of the game.

Variations

⊕ The game can be played in teams to accommodate more players.

⊕ Use the Concentration template on page 71 to make your own Concentration game.

hot

cold

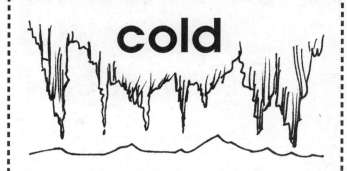

big

little

happy

sad

thin

thick

in

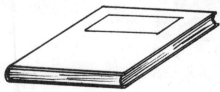

out

front

back

 **tall**

short

 **asleep**

awake

white

black

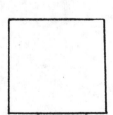 **night**

day

Rhyming Words Relay

This game is ideal for rainy or other bad weather days. It is a modified relay race. It gets children up and moving in a controlled way!

Objective: To practice finding words that rhyme.

Players: up to 5 teams of 3 or 4 children each

Materials: chalkboard or white board, and a piece of chalk or white board marker for each team

Preparation: Print team headings and sample rhyming words on the board as shown below. You may wish to review rhyming words.

```
TEAM 1      TEAM 2      TEAM 3
cat         mill        fan
1.  mat     1. hill     1.  can
2.          2.          2.
3.          3.          3.
4.          4.          4.
```

To Play the Game

1. Divide the class into teams. If there are more than 20 children in the class, you can divide the class into two sets of teams and play two sets of games, one after the other.

2. Have the teams stand in lines about five feet away from the board. Give the first player of each team a piece of chalk or a marker.

3. When you say, "On your mark. . . Get set. . .Go!" the first player of each team runs to the board. The child reads the word aloud and then prints a word that rhymes with it. For example, s/he could write the word *mat* under the word *cat*.

4. The first players then take the marker or chalk to the second players, who repeat the process with a different word that rhymes. This continues with the other team members.

5. The winning team is the first to have completed its list of rhyming words.

Sample Words That Have Word Families

mat	mad	bed
pot	gold	mill
nest	hay	can
sent	chin	lip
tack	seat	tall

Word-Match Dominoes

This game is a variation of dominoes. Instead of matching up dots, students match words that rhyme.

Objective: To practice identifying rhyming words.

Players: 2 to 4 children

Materials: rhyming-word dominoes

Preparation: Cut out, or have students cut out the dominoes.

To Play the Game

1 Shuffle the dominoes and place them facedown on a table or desk. Have each player take five dominoes.

2 A player with a double domino (the same picture at both ends) places the double domino in the center of the table.

3 Players add dominoes in turn. Each player checks his or her dominoes to see if any of them match either end of the domino(es) on the table. A domino matches if (a) it has the same picture, or (b) has a picture of an object that rhymes with the pictured object. (For example, a domino with a goat at one end and a hen at the other could be added to an end domino that shows another goat, another hen, a coat, a boat, a pen, or men.)

4 If a player cannot add a domino to either end, s/he draws another domino from the pile and waits for the next turn.

5 The player who runs out of dominoes first is the winner.

20 Fun-Filled Games That Build Early Reading Skills Scholastic Professional Books

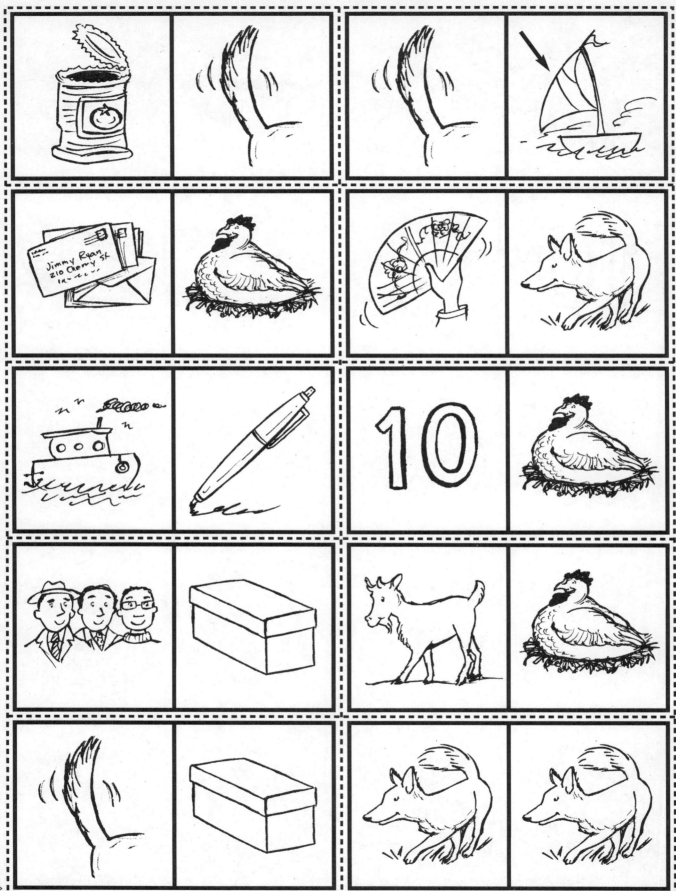

Word-Match Dominoes

Vowel Dice Toss

**This game combines learning vowel sounds
with the fun of playing with dice.**

Objective: To practice identifying short and long vowels.

To practice making words with short and long vowels.

Players: 2 to 6 children

Materials: vowel dice template, scissors, and glue

Preparation: Use the reproducible dice cut-out to make long-vowel and short-vowel dice. Follow the directions on the page.

To Play the Game

1 Place the long- and short-vowel dice in a bag.

2 Have the first player pick out a die and toss it.

3 If the die shows a vowel, the child must say a word containing that vowel. For example, if the short vowel *a* appears, the student could say, "Short vowel *a*. The word *cat* has the short *a* vowel." The child scores one point for identifying the short *a* vowel and one point for identifying a word with the short *a* vowel, for a total of two points.

4 If the die shows **Skip a Turn** the child scores no points. If the die shows **3 Bonus Points**, s/he scores three points.

5 Continue with the rest of the players. You may have the children play one round or several. The winner is the child with the most points at the end of the game.

Variations

✤ The dice pieces can be mounted on tagboard or heavy-weight construction paper.

Long-Vowel Die

GLUE

GLUE

3 Bonus Points

GLUE

GLUE

ā   ē   ī   ō

GLUE

GLUE

ū

GLUE

GLUE

Preparing the Dice

1. Photocopy this page.

2. Cut out along the dotted lines.

3. Fold along the dotted lines and glue where indicated.

GLUE

GLUE

Skip a Turn

GLUE

ă   ĕ   ĭ   ŏ

GLUE

GLUE

GLUE

ŭ

GLUE

Short-Vowel Die

Collaborative Crossword Puzzle

This game is based on the concept of crossword puzzles. Dolch words are printed vertically on one side of a strip of paper and horizontally on the other side. Students use the strips to build a crossword.

Objectives: To practice reading simple Dolch words.

Players: 2 to 4 children

Materials: crossword puzzle strips sheet (on the reproducible)

Preparation: Photocopy the puzzle strips on page 65. Cut along the dotted lines. Then, fold along the dotted lines. Glue the white-facing sides together, forming puzzle strips that may be used on the horizontal or vertical.

To Play the Game

1 Have each player take four strips. Put the remaining strips in a pile.

2 Explain that the purpose of the game is to play all of one's word strips as quickly as possible by fitting its letters to those in other strips.

3 The player with the longest word begins by reading it aloud and then placing the strip with the horizontal word faceup on the table.

4 The next player places another word on one of the letters of the first word so that it builds the beginning of a crossword. For example, if the first word is *pretty* horizontally, the second player could use *there* vertically by placing the *t* over one of the *t*'s in *pretty*. If a student cannot play any word, he or she draws a strip from the pile. Students must read each word aloud before they place it on the crossword.

5 Each added word must fit the words already on the table. It must make a word with any letters it touches.

6 The first student to use all of his or her strips is the winner.

Variation

- Students can make their own crossword games using the Crossword-Builder Grid on page 70.

Note: The upper levels of Dolch words were chosen because they are slightly longer than the earlier levels of Dolch words. This game works better with longer words than with shorter ones.

p	r	e	t	t	y

c	a	m	e

p	l	e	a	s	e

f	o	u	r

b	l	a	c	k

t	h	e	r	e

t	h	i	n	k

g	o	o	d	fold

t	h	a	n	k

h	a	v	e	fold

t	h	o	s	e

m	u	s	t	fold

u	n	d	e	r		i	n	t	o

fold

w	h	i	t	e		l	i	k	e

fold

t	h	e	s	e		r	i	d	e

fold

s	o	o	n		t	h	a	t

fold

t	h	e	y		t	h	i	s

fold

w	a	n	t		w	e	l	l

fold

w	h	a	t	s	o	m	e

fold

w	h	a	t	s	o	m	e

w	a	l	k	w	e	e	k

fold

w	a	l	k	w	e	e	k

t	a	k	e	w	o	r	k

fold

t	a	k	e	w	o	r	k

t	a	l	e	w	i	s	h

fold

t	a	l	e	w	i	s	h

w	h	e	n	w	a	s	h

fold

w	h	e	n	w	a	s	h

20 Fun-Filled Games That Build Early Reading Skills Scholastic Professional Books

Letter-Sound Bingo Cards

	FREE	

Letter-Sound Bingo Cards

	FREE	

Letter-Sound Bingo Cards

	FREE	

Letter-Sound Bingo Cards

	FREE	

Letter-Sound Bingo Cards

	FREE	

Letter-Sound Bingo Cards

	FREE	

Concentration Cards Template

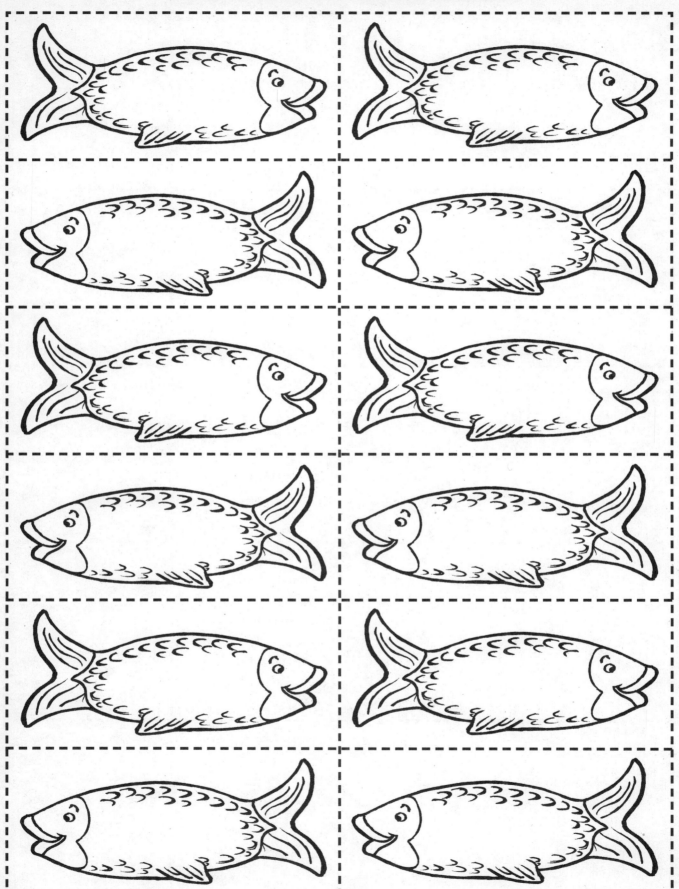